This bite-sized book has been designed to give you a simplified and useful overview of sleep and how you can get the best rest.

It will help you to:

- Understand sleep and how it works
- Learn about the benefits of quality sleep
- Improve your overall well-being through sleep
- Manage your stress levels more effectively
- Feel refreshed and energised

Please note that this bite-sized book does not replace the advice of a medical professional, however it does offer a few useful suggestions that can help you. All research sources have been curated on page 33 of this book.

GW00707805

3

The best bridge between despair and hope is a good night's sleep

E. Joseph Cossman

Sleep in the modern ages

The non-stop pace of modern life and the 24/7 connectivity can make getting a good night's sleep challenging.

In some work cultures there can be a tendency to even boast about late night working and lack of sleep as a proud testament of productivity and commitment to work.

An increasing amount of evidence however shows, in no uncertain terms, that lack of sleep is nothing to brag about. Infact, a chronic lack of sleep can bring about a whole host of medical issues.

Scientific research from various universities around the world has identified that lack of quality sleep can increase your risk of disease and elevate blood pressure. It can also have a very negative impact on your emotional well-being by exacerbating depression, triggering anxiety and amplifying irritability and mood swings.

Getting the right amount of sleep for you plays a big part in looking after your mental health.

Without enough sleep, we all
become tall two-year-olds

Jojo Jensen

We are all unique

Every person is different in terms of the amount of sleep that they need and there is no magic number of hours set in stone.

An increasing amount of studies have shown that the amount of sleep people actually need is unique to each individual. This will vary with age and also your level of activity and amount of energy you exert throughout the day.

How much sleep you actually need will also vary throughout your lifetime depending on your age and circumstances.

The common consensus is that lack of quality sleep can have a profound effect on your physical and emotional well-being. It is important to identify how much sleep you personally require so that you can function at your best throughout the day.

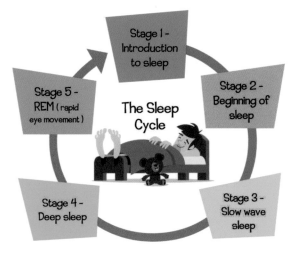

The Sleep Cycle

Stage 1 - Introduction to sleep

Stage 2 - Beginning of sleep

Stage 3 - Slow wave sleep

Stage 4 - Deep sleep

Stage 5 - REM (rapid eye movement)

And so to sleep ...

During sleep, the body moves through five different stages of both NREM (non-rapid eye movement) and REM (rapid eye movement) sleep.

Throughout the night, your body will go through the five-stage sleep cycle around four to six times, spending an average of ninety minutes in each cycle.

Each stage of the sleep cycle serves as a unique restorative function. This includes muscle recovery, hormone regulation and memory consolidation.

Without a full night of sleep, your body and mind will be deprived of the essential elements needed to help you to be at your best during the following day.

Sleep improves your memory

An increasing area of interest in the field of neuroscience is the potential link between sleep and memory. Growing evidence supports the idea that specific stages of sleep have a beneficial effect on memory.

Your memory plays such a big role in your life. It allows you to remember skills that you have learnt, retrieve information that is stored in the brain and recall precious moments that occurred in the past.

Sleep helps you make better choices

Lack of sleep leads to a compromised ability to focus and make decisions. After too little sleep it becomes difficult to properly regulate the parts of your brain associated with consciousness, alertness and decision-making.

Being alert and on the ball plays a huge part in being productive both at work and home.

It is also essential to be alert for your own personal safety and the safety of others. Making intelligent choices is much more difficult when you are tired and lack focus.

It is a common experience that a problem difficult at night is resolved in the morning after the committee of sleep has worked on it

John Steinbeck

Sleep boosts your creativity

A recent study at Cardiff University showed that Stage 5 of the sleep cycle known as REM sleep boosts creativity. This stage promotes creative ways of thinking about the memories that you consolidate in non-REM sleep.

It may seem counter-intuitive, however the best way to get your mind working may be to put it to sleep. Lots of great innovators have shared how some of their best ideas came to them either in a dream or upon waking.

Sleep reduces stress

Stress levels can increase when the length and quality of sleep decreases. Sometimes you may find yourself lying in bed worrying and feeling anxious, which can make it almost impossible to relax enough to fall asleep.

The brain chemicals connected with deep sleep tell the body to stop the production of stress hormones. When you don't sleep well, your body keeps producing those hormones. The next day, you may end up feeling even more stressed and then the following night you find it harder to fall asleep, and so the cycle continues.

Sleep is for champions

The myth of working ridiculously long hours to be a success in the workplace has been broken. There is so much more focus now on working smarter not harder.

Those who demonstrate a commitment to personal well-being and self-care win far more respect. Looking after yourself through a healthy diet, exercising and getting enough rest will also build your resilience.

You are a human being not a human doing and everyone needs to take valuable time to recharge and replenish.

How to sleep well

1. Keep regular sleeping hours

Your circadian rhythm is a 24-hour internal clock that is running in the background of your brain and cycles between sleepiness and alertness at regular intervals. It functions on a set loop, aligning itself with sunrise and sunset.

Being consistent with your sleep and waking times can aid long-term sleep quality. Irregular sleep patterns can alter your circadian rhythm and levels of melatonin, which signal your brain to sleep.

If you struggle with your sleep, get in the habit of waking up and going to bed at similar times. After several weeks, you may not even need an alarm.

2. Exercise

Exercise is great for sleep, as well as for your health generally. Exercise is a beneficial stressor to the body. The brain compensates for the physical stress by increasing the amount of time you spend in deep sleep.

Exercise also encourages sleep because it causes your body temperature to rise and then fall by an equal amount a few hours later. This drop in your body temperature makes it easier to fall asleep and stay asleep.

3. Relax

There are lots of things that you can do to relax before you go to bed. Here are 3 top tips:

1. Focus on your breathing
Take a deep breath into your stomach and then out through your nose, making your out-breath longer than your in-breath. You can keep repeating this until you feel relaxed.

2. Progressively relax your muscles
You can do this by consciously tensing each muscle and relaxing them, one after the other. Starting with your toes and working your way up through your body until you reach the top of your head.

3. Listen to music
Music has many therapeutic benefits and listening to calming music can help relieve stress and anxiety. It may also improve your mood and help with your overall well-being.
The Sleep Foundation proposes classical or jazz songs with 60 to 80 beats per minute as the best recommendations for your sleep playlist.

TOP
3
TIPS

4. Soak before you sleep

A pre-bedtime soak can be very relaxing whether that is in the bath or taking a shower. Epsom salts are great for detoxification and relieving stress as well as natural sleep-inducing scents and herbs like lavender, camomile, and magnesium.

Going from warm water into a cooler bedroom will cause your body temperature to drop, naturally making you feel sleepy.

Sleep is the best meditation

Dalai Lama

5. Practise mindfulness

Mindfulness is a mental state achieved by focusing your awareness on the present moment, while calmly acknowledging and accepting your feelings, thoughts and bodily sensations.

Meditation programmes such as Mindfulness-Based Stress Reduction (MBSR) have been shown to be effective in treating sleep disorders. A research team in the Netherlands has also identified that even a small amount of mindfulness meditation can help calm a hyperactive mind and improve the quality of sleep.

Man should forget his anger
before he lies down to sleep

Mahatma Gandhi

6. Write it down

When you have things on your mind that are perhaps making you anxious it is best to get them off your chest. Lying in bed and festering about things that may have upset you and playing them over and over in your mind can build up unnecessary stress.

A useful tip is to write down what is on your mind and create a cons and pros list. First of all write down what is bothering you and then flip it over and think about a positive solution or identify the potential opportunity in the situation.

It is also good to keep a gratitude journal and write down three things at the end of the day that were positive highlights. By focusing on these before you go to sleep you will drift off in a positive and happy frame of mind.

7. Switch off

Ideally your bedroom needs to be somewhere that you associate with sleep. Wherever possible, remove distractions. It is far better to watch TV, check social media and eat in another room.

An increasing amount of sleep advice suggests keeping technology out of the bedroom altogether. The backlit 'blue light' displays on some gadgets suppress melatonin production which is the hormone that helps you sleep.

The suppression of melatonin can cause sleep disruption during the night too, so the sooner you switch off technology before you go to sleep, the better.

8. Avoid stimulants

Some substances can disrupt your sleep cycles because of the energy spike and ensuing crash you get that can play havoc with your body clock. Spicy and sugary foods, alcohol and large meals are best not to be consumed before you go to bed.

Caffeine ingested too close to bedtime will make it more difficult for you to get to sleep. Alcohol, on the other hand, tends to ruin the second half of your night's sleep. When you drink before you go to bed, about halfway through the night, your body starts to process the alcohol, and then it begins to act as a stimulant and wakes you up.

Various research has also shown that, if you don't sleep well, you may demonstrate a tendency to turn to junk food the next day, creating a cycle of poor sleep and bad diet.

A lovely soothing cup of camomile tea is a far better way to end the day.

Nothing cures insomnia like
the realization that it's
time to get up

Author Unknown

9. Avoid clock watching

Worrying about getting enough sleep can itself stop you sleeping. The best way to deal with this is to remind yourself that resting in bed and focusing on positive and pleasant thoughts is more productive than tossing and turning and looking at your alarm clock every few minutes. Occasional loss of sleep is not going to hurt you so getting worked up about it is not going to help.

If you find you simply cannot sleep then get up and do something you find relaxing until you feel sleepy again, then go back to bed.

If lack of sleep is persistent and it is affecting your daily life in a negative way it may be advisable to book an appointment to see your doctor, naturopath or a sleep specialist.

At the end of the day,
sleep is a barometer of
your emotional health

Mehmet Oz

10. Create a sanctuary for sleep

Here are five useful tips to create a sanctuary for sleep:

1. Invest in a good quality mattress which will ensure your bed provides the correct support, comfort and space.

2. Declutter your bedroom and keep it tidy. If you look at chaos before you go to sleep it will agitate you and create anxiety.

3. Get a diffuser to create pleasant smells, such as lavender and geranium, which can be really soothing.

4. Make sure that your bedroom is the right temperature, somewhere between 16 °C and 18 °C (60°F to 65°F) ideally.

5. Block out any light as this is essential for sleep and the absence of light sends a critical signal to your body that it is time to rest. Light exposure throughout the night can lead to frequent and prolonged awakenings so invest in blackout curtains or blinds if necessary.

The machinery is always going.
Even when you sleep

Andy Warhol

If you are looking for more in-depth advice these websites are very helpful and have been curated for the excellent advice they offer around sleep.

www.thriveglobal.com

www.mentalhealth.org.uk

www.sleepfoundation.org

www.sleepcouncil.org.uk

www.nhs.uk/live-well

www.sleepassociation.org

www.mind.org.uk

www.healthline.com

www.helpforheroes.org.uk

www.hse.gov.uk

A good laugh and a long sleep
are the best cures in
the doctor's book

Irish proverb